Zen Without
Zen Masters

OTHER TITLES FROM NEW FALCON PUBLICATIONS

ZEN
WITHOUT
ZEN MASTERS

By Camden Benares

Commentary By
Robert Anton Wilson

Illustrated by
Deborah M. Cotter

NEW FALCON PUBLICATIONS
TEMPE, ARIZONA, U.S.A.

International Standard Book Number: 1-56184-073-4
Library of Congress Catalog Card Number: 85-70387

First Edition 1977 (And/Or Press)
Second Printing 1978
Third Printing 1978
First Falcon Edition 1985
Second Printing 1988
Third Printing 1990
Fourth Printing 1993
Fifth Printing 2004

The paper used in this publication meets the minimum requirements of the American National Standard for Permanence of Paper for Printed Library Materials Z39.48-1984

Address all inquiries to:
NEW FALCON PUBLICATIONS
1739 East Broadway Road #1-277
Tempe, AZ 85282 U.S.A.
(or)
320 East Charleston Blvd. #204-286
Las Vegas, NV 89104 U.S.A.

website: http://www.newfalcon.com
email: info@newfalcon.com

For Kerry Thornley and Gregory Hill

PREFACE

In my search for an understanding of Zen, some of my first questions were: What is Zen? What can it do for me? How do I get into it? The following statements are my current best answers to those questions.

Zen is the radical approach to Buddhism. Historically, Zen arose as a Buddhist sect resulting from a blend of Buddhism and Taoism. According to some traditions, Zen came into being with the meeting of Buddha and Lao Tse about 2,500 years ago. However, most authorities believe Zen developed in China in the sixth century of the common era when Indian Buddhist missionaries encountered Taoists. Zen spread to Japan via China and Korea in the twelfth and thirteenth centuries, and from Japan to the West at the beginning of the twentieth century.

What Zen has done for me is to clarify and liberate my state of consciousness. Zen offered a way of experiencing life directly, a way of learning who I was and how I wanted to live.

There are two approaches to getting into Zen. The formal approach is to study with a Japanese Zen Master. The informal approach is an individual study program using whatever materials are available. The informal approach results in what I call Western Zen. I see it as the next step in the radical Zen tradition. *Zen Without Zen Masters* represents my attempt to share Western Zen with you.

This book may create questions in the minds of some readers. Are the Zen stories real? Many of the stories, including some of the most improbable sounding ones, are taken verbatim from life. Others are real events revised and edited for a more meaningful presentation. A few are based on hearsay from sources that vary in reliability. A small minority are Zen in parable form.

Do the exercises and meditation guides work? To the best of my knowledge and experience, they do. This doesn't mean that they will work for everyone at all times. Your experience should be your guide. I have no wish for you to do anything that doesn't produce results for you.

What is the purpose of this book? My words about Zen are intended to aid you in "getting more out of life." But neither these words nor their meaning is Zen, because Zen is the reality behind the meaning. This book is one tool to help you experience that reality in its fullness.

TABLE OF CONTENTS

COMMENTARY

Say the magic word and the duck will come down and pay you $100.

—Marx

Many readers of *Illuminatus* have asked me why Hagbard Celine used the letters "H.M." and "S.H." after his name and what these mysterious initials meant. I have always evaded these questions in the past because I was not at all sure that Hagbard wanted this story revealed. However, in *Zen Without Zen Masters,* Camden Benares has blatantly disclosed all the inner secrets of mysticism and he even reveals the early incident in Hagbard's life from which the initials "H.M." and "S.H." derive. The story is called "Enlightenment of a Seeker" and is on page 40.

Others have often asked me if all the characters in *Illuminatus* really existed. Indeed they do. The enigmatic Malaclypse the Younger in *Illuminatus* is the same individual as "Mal" in *Zen Without Zen Masters.* (See, for instance, "Mal's Truth" on page 18.)

The philosophy expressed in this book—also called "Discordianism" or "Erisianism" or even "Marxism-Lennonism"*—is a group artwork, like reality itself. Camden Benares didn't invent it anymore than I did, or Mal did, or Ho Chi Zen did. Like Topsy in *Uncle Tom's Cabin,* or the universe around us, it "jes' grew."

Some say that the first Erisian atheologian was Zeno of Elias who proved that an arrow can never hit its target (because first it must travel half the distance to the target, and before that it must travel half of that distance or ¼ the original distance, and before that it must travel half of that distance—or 1/8 of the original—etc., to infinity).

Others say the first Erisian was really Sri Syadasti, the Hindu sage who announced that all affirmations are true in some sense, false in some sense, meaningless in some sense, true and false in some sense, true and meaningless in some sense, false and meaningless in some sense, and true and false and meaningless in some sense. But this is denied by those who claim Sri Syadasti is not to be found in Hindu scripture

---

*Named after Groucho and John, of course. A basic Discordian koan is "Why *don't* we do it in the road?"

and was actually invented by the mischievous Ho Chi Zen.

It does seem fairly well documented that an Erisian missionary arrived in the Bay Area of California in 1849 and took the name Norton I, with the title "Emperor of the United States and Protector of Mexico." Norton was immediately recognized as an Illuminated Being by the foremost occult order in San Francisco, the Ancient and Accepted Freemasons, who granted him a 33° and buried him, at his death in 1880, in the masonic cemetery.

It is fairly well established that, although a pauper, Norton I was allowed to dine sumptuously in the best restaurants of San Francisco; although a lunatic, he wrote letters which were seriously considered by such folk as Abraham Lincoln and Queen Victoria; and, although a charlatan, he was so beloved that 30,000 turned out for his funeral.

When the Committee of Vigilance, in an impetuous mood, set out to burn down Chinatown on one occasion, Norton I dispersed them by merely standing in the street, head bowed, praying. As Lao-Tse says, "When the proper man does nothing (wu-wei) his thought is felt 10,000 miles."

Malaclypse the Younger has indicated Norton I's importance, writing in his infamous *Principia Discordia,* "Everybody understands Mickey Mouse. Few understand Hermann Hesse. Hardly anybody understands Einstein. And nobody understands Emperor Norton." Mordecai the Foul, High Priest of the Head Temple of the Bavarian Illuminati, says of Norton with simple awe, "Live like him!"

What is the central truth behind Marxism-Lennonism, Erisianism, Discordianism, Zen Without Zen Masters? On this point, our leading atheologians are in agreement—and disagreement (as might be expected). Mal says, simply, "God is a crazy woman and Her name is Eris." Ho says more abstractly and less figuratively, "Hell is reserved exclusively for them that belive in it." Camden says concisely, "If we believe enough, there will be whatamores. Do we really want any?" Mordecai the Foul merely exclaims "Fnord!" and hits you with a stick if you ask again.

But, seriously, folks (as Bob Hope always says) *Zen Without Zen Masters,* like all the other aspects of Operation Mindfuck, is not a complicated joke disguised as a new form of Buddhism. It is a new form of Buddhism disguised as a complicated joke. Guerilla ontology. Epistemological judo. If you don't laugh at all, you've missed the point. If you *only* laugh, you've missed your chance for Illumination. As Lichtenberg said elsewhere, "This book is a mirror. If a monkey looks in, no philosopher looks out."

Hail Eris!

OM!

Fnord?

—*Robert Anton Wilson*

I. Guides and Lovable Fools

SOLITARY SYSTEM

There are many individuals who are liberated or who appear to be so. Some of them seek disciples because they have not heeded Nietzsche, who said, "What? You seek followers? You would multiply yourself by ten, by a hundred, by a thousand? Seek zeroes!" Remember this and know that any system of liberation may work once, for one individual.

MASTERS AND TEACHERS

When asked about masters and teachers, Ho Chi Zen always had this to say: "The Old Fox can learn more from the Young Fool than the Young Fool can ever hope to learn from the Old Fox."

MAL'S TRUTH

When an interviewer asked Mal if his teaching was serious or humorous, Mal replied, "Sometimes I take humor seriously and sometimes I take seriousness humorously. Either way it is irrelevant."

The interviewer responded by proposing that Mal was crazy. Mal grinned and said, "Indeed! But don't reject these teachings just because I am crazy. I am crazy because they are true."

BEN AND THE FANATIC

In his teachings, Ben stressed that Zen was his path because it allowed him to become himself. All the other routes that allegedly lead to cosmic consciousness seemed to put him in conflict with his own nature. He advised all seekers to examine carefully what each system asked of the potential initiate, keeping in mind three rules:

1. What you are required to believe is what the system cannot prove.
2. Anything that you are asked to keep secret is of more value to the teacher than to the student.
3. Any practice that is forbidden offers something that the system cannot successfully replace with an alternative.

One listener asked, "Don't you believe that giving up the pleasures of the senses will produce a different consciousness?"

"My personal experience," Ben replied, "was that it produced the consciousness of fanaticism."

AUDIENCE RESPONSE

Ben was once asked how he expected anyone to take some of his teachings seriously when they provoked so much laughter from his listeners. He replied, "Laughter is the only genuine form of applause."

A COMMON DISEASE

By surrounding himself with true believers, Waldo fell into the trap of taking himself too seriously. This led to unhappiness and ill health. When he asked Ralph, one of the few who had penetrated his multilevel cover stories, what he thought the problem was, Ralph replied, "You're suffering from hardening of the orthodoxies."

POP QUIZ

Ralph, like many others in the rascal guru tradition, exploits the credulousness of his students as much for his own amusement as for their edification. When anyone asks how he accumulated so much wisdom, he usually pulls their leg by implying that he has been here for several centuries. Swallowing that statement without a gulp, one student replied, "It's amazing how human you are." Without a pause Ralph responded, "After a thousand years or so you go native."

HO CHI ZEN'S SCHOOL

When Ho Chi Zen decided to take students, he put a bowl for donations just inside the door. Over the small brass container was a sign that read: If you wish to donate, do so before class.

Habitually, Ho Chi Zen stood where he could see which student donated and which student did not as they entered. Asked why he did so, Ho explained, "Any student who contributes three times in a row is dismissed for excessive gullibility."

DR. ZEN

Omar was associated with a very unusual black man whom he referred to as Dr. Zen. Anyone who tuned in on Dr. Zen thought he was either crazy or very detached. Omar believed that Dr. Zen was quite literally a Christian Zen practitioner.

When Omar learned that Dr. Zen advertised himself as a Biblical analyst, he asked him how many times he had read the Bible. "Oh," he answered, "I've never read the Bible. I don't need to read it. If you understand just one verse in the Bible, you understand it all."

An onlooker asked, "Which verse is that?"

Dr. Zen replied, "Jesus wept."

A RINGING IN THE EARS

A celibate member of a traditional Zen sect once asked Ho Chi Zen if he had taken any vows.

"After the Great Acceptance has been made," Ho replied, "all vows tinkle like tin bells."

HYPOC'S EARRING

During a social evening at Hypoc's home, Mal, commenting on the gold earring Hypoc wears in his left ear, asked if anyone knew why a single earring, when worn, is invariably worn in the left ear. Bert said that merchant seamen wear an earring in the left ear to signify that they have crossed the equator.

This led into a discussion concerning the possible symbolic significance of a mystical crossing of a personal equator. The talk touched on other points such as the left ear representing the individual freedom found on the left side of conformity and of the association of the left ear with the occult.

When the discussion waned, Mal asked Hypoc why he wore the earring in his left ear. Hypoc replied, "I like to sleep on my right ear."

LUCAS'S MEDITATION

After learning transcendental meditation, Lucas taught the simple techniques to anyone who expressed an interest. Unlike many meditation teachers, he charged no money, asking only that meditators give him something of value in return for his time. Instead of an elaborate ritual in a foreign language, Lucas gave a quiet talk on the way to empty the mind of its chatter while candles burned and incense filled the room. One learner asked, "Why should I empty my mind?" Lucas, rephrasing Lao Tse, replied, "Wheels without empty centers cannot be used to haul, and the empty part of the bowl makes it useful for holding food."

OTIS AND THE OLDER STUDENT

An older student came to Otis and said, "I have been to see a great number of teachers and I have given up a great number of pleasures. I have fasted, been celibate and stayed awake nights seeking enlightenment. I have given up everything I was asked to give up and I have suffered, but I have not been enlightened. What should I do?"

Otis replied, "Give up suffering."

PETER AND THE JAPANESE ZEN MASTER

Peter, an actor and teacher, went to a Zen lecture on the campus where he taught. A philosophy professor introduced the speaker, a Japanese Zen Master, and the speaker's associate. Speaking in English, the Zen Master announced that he would deliver the lecture in Japanese and that it would be translated into English by his associate, who had a better command of English. Peter asked the Zen Master to speak in English, saying that the Zen Master's English was excellent and that the associate could clarify any confusion during the discussion period.

Looking at Peter, the Zen Master asked, "Who are you?"

Peter replied, "I am an actor."

The Zen Master said, "Then you act," and left the lecture room.

THE ZEN TEMPLE ATTENDANT

Jefferson went through despair, came out on the other side, and began to develop a new life. He spent his time taking care of his body and mind as one, instead of two. When he learned that there was a Zen temple near, he went to it and presented himself. The attendant told Jefferson to go home because the proper time for new students to come was posted. He said, "Now is not the time. I am not ready to receive a new student." Jefferson knew that now is the only time and he understood that the attendant wasn't ready.

HO'S FIRST SERMON

By listening carefully to the words of teachers and leaders of all kinds and then more or less doing as I pleased, by avoiding both belief and doubt, and by letting my desires and attachments tumble out in whatever order they attained among themselves, I have managed quite resolutely to overcome all temptations and remain in accord with the Tao.

But it hasn't been easy, for the Path climbs a steep, slippery rock and meanders incessantly. And also one never knows but what the Buddhas and patriarchs were not the fools they must have been. Besides, the True Way could be as inorganically straight and narrow as they insisted.

Yet the Perfect Seer will persist in the knowledge that any road traveled in harmlessness and devotion is the Peerless Instructor.

GLADYS AND THE ZEN MASTER

In her search for Zen, Gladys went to a Japanese mona-
stery where she spent several months. Continually asking the
Zen Master, "What is Zen?" she received no answer.

To show how humble she was, Gladys cleaned the com-
munal bathrooms. The Zen Master was not impressed and she
felt humiliated.

When Gladys realized that if she wanted to clean bathrooms she could do that anywhere, she decided to leave. She
told the Zen Master of her decision. He replied, "That is Zen."

ADVANCE FROM THE RETREAT

Looking for personal growth, Jane went to a rural retreat for a few weeks. The fee she paid entitled her to room and board plus instructions from a guru. As in many such places, students were used as slave labor for the good of the guru, who would tell them their labors were for their development. When Jane felt that she had nothing more to learn from manual labor, she told the guru that his training program was a masochist's delight—an all day suffer. He responded with "You must get beyond pleasure." Jane answered, "If you think you can get beyond pleasure without going through it, we are definitely on different trips," and left.

THE ARTIST'S ENLIGHTENMENT

An artist, depressed and almost unable to paint, consulted Sam, a Zen-oriented therapist, for aid in coping with his problems. He asked what the fee would be, explaining that his income had dwindled since he was doing fewer paintings. Sam said his fee would be two paintings. The first, to be titled *Despair,* was to be completed before the therapy began; the second was to be titled by the artist and was to be started when the therapy ended.

The artist painted *Despair* and presented it to Sam, who looked at it and then threw it into the blazing fireplace. The artist walked out. He returned a few days later with the second painting.

EXPENSIVE ADVICE

Omar and Giovanni were planning a joint venture that looked as if it might make them both some money. Having a genuine horror toward what middle class money does to most people, Omar hesitated and asked, "What the hell will I do if this scheme makes me rich? I'm not eager to handle that."

Giovanni replied, "Omar, I've always given you lots of advice that you've never taken. If you get rich, I'll just start giving you expensive advice. You can take it, have lots of interesting experiences and get rid of money."

"That sounds good, but give me a concrete example. Let's say I had fifteen thousand dollars to get rid of. What should I do?"

"You know that famous guru who's hung up on fast cars? Okay, you buy the Italian sports car I was looking at yesterday. Then we drive down to where he lives. When he comes to the door, you give him the keys and say, 'This is your new car. We hope you enjoy it,' and then we walk off. He'll call us back for an explanation and we'll tell him it's his with no strings attached. Then he'll say 'Isn't there something I can do for you.' You'll look thoughtful and say, 'Well, there is one thing. Could you drop us off at the nearest bus stop?' "

VOTING

Smitty described the following voting system to Omar: Each candidate would have a yes and a no box after his or her name, allowing each voter a choice between voting for a candidate or voting against another one. Each negative vote would cancel a positive vote. This, Smitty explained, would prevent a politician who was elected from assuming he had a mandate just because a few voters found him a better gamble. When he asked Omar what he thought of the system, Omar replied, "I never vote. It only encourages them."

THE RIGHT TO DIE

A potential suicide was talking to Ho Chi Zen, asking if he had the right to commit suicide if he wanted to. Ho replied, "Anyone has a right to do anything. Every one else has the right to resist it."

The student said, "Do you see suicide as a moral act?"

Ho's answer was, "Where there is no victim, every act is morally right, but I personally think suicide is a symptom of taking oneself too seriously."

OBSTACLES

Giovanni told Omar that he was interested in Zen but there were two obstacles in his path to liberation through Zen: one, he couldn't understand most of what he had read about Zen; two, he didn't believe that he could bring himself to make all the changes he felt he would have to make in his actions if he embraced Zen.

Omar told him to read Alan Watts' books on Zen and then reread everything that he hadn't understood before. "That will take care of the first obstacle," Omar said, "and the second is merely an obstacle illusion. You do not make your actions conform to some arbitrary standard. Your actions reflect you. In Zen, you and your actions are one."

THE PRIEST

An actor picked up a hitchhiker who revealed that he was a Catholic priest who had left the Church. Explaining his current situation, the former cleric said, "I'm living with a woman. I love her and we want to get married. This morning two representatives of the church came to where I live. They told me to appear at a hearing in San Francisco to determine my relationship to the Church. I told them that I'm doing God's will, but they didn't believe me. Do you believe me?"

The actor replied, "Yes, I believe you. As part of my preparation to become an actor, I studied Zen. One of the things I learned is that if God's actions appear irrational and inconsistent, you must remember that he is playing to the broadest possible audience."

ENLIGHTENMENT OF A SEEKER

A serious young man found the conflicts of mid twentieth century America confusing. He went to many people seeking a way of resolving the discords that troubled him, but he remained troubled.

One night in a coffee house, a self-ordained Zen minister said to him, "Go to the dilapidated mansion you will find at the address which I have written down for you. Do not speak to those who live there: you must remain silent until the moon rises tomorrow night. Go to the large room on the right of the main hallway, sit in the lotus position on top of the rubble in the northeast corner, face the corner and meditate.

He did as the Zen minister instructed. His meditation was frequently interrupted by worries. He worried whether or not the rest of the plumbing fixtures would fall from the second floor to join the pipes and other trash he was sitting on. He worried how would he know when the moon rose on the next night. He worried about what the people who walked through the room said about him.

His worrying and meditation were disturbed when, as if in a test of his faith, effluvium fell from the second floor onto him. At that time two people walked into the room. The first asked the second who the man sitting there was. The second replied "Some say he is a holy man. Others say he is a shithead."

Hearing this, the man was enlightened.

HO CHI ZEN CONFIDES AGAIN

Asked what was the purpose of Zen, Ho said, "By the study of Zen one can learn to help people—or, that failing, at least to get them off your back."

II. Personal Work

PERSONAL WORK

The most important work you will ever do is upon yourself. Any occupation you engage in can be used for that purpose, but not necessarily for a lifetime. Since most of us select from visible alternatives, we avoid confronting our fears and become what we are least afraid of becoming. Now is the time to understand those fears so we can get on with our personal work.

LIVING ZEN

I have made all the right choices—I chose the right path based on my ability to choose.

I am in the right place; there is no other place for me to live my life and I could not live the life of another—for it would not fit; it would not remain another's life, but become mine.

INSTANT ENLIGHTENMENT

That sudden awareness—the awakening of the Buddha within—can come in an instant. The experience might be triggered by a concept, a word, an event, a koan, a meditation or anything else perceived in its fullness. It's quite a bit like the overnight success in show business: it's frequently preceded by years of hard work.

FOCUS

You are personally responsible for your continued existence. There are many ways of focusing your attention elsewhere, but to really experience your life, the focus must be on you as the center of the perceived universe. You may devote as much time as you wish to causes as long as you don't use them as an excuse for trying to change others instead of yourself. Anytime that you are doing something that you think is not for you, re-examine both your thinking and your actions. If it isn't for you, you're fooling yourself or doing it wrong.

CHANGE

Life is a continuing process of change. Resistance to change and personal growth is one of the most difficult ways to attempt to live because it requires a denial of the process. One of the hazards of refusing to accept change in yourself is getting locked into the habit of trying to change others so you can have the illusion of remaining the same. That way of living will take all your energy and yield no personal returns. Why waste your energy on changing others? You can use it to flow with the changes that are happening to you and enjoy the unfolding of your own life.

PRALAYA'S WISDOM

Having had a vision that revealed that he would travel to truth by an unexpected path, Pralaya investigated several blind alleys in a quest for liberation. Asked how he avoided discouragement, he said, "In learning the yoga of tying shoe laces with the teeth, one must accept that sometimes the foot will be in the mouth."

WHO'S IN CHARGE HERE?

You are the creator of the reality that you experience. Every event that occurs around you takes on meaning when you put your attention on it. During your lifetime you have been exposed to a lot of conditioning, but you have selected what seemed valid to you and made it part of your programming. If reality is getting you down, examine the programming that is in the biocomputer you call your mind. That programming can be changed at any time because you are your own programmer.

RESPONSIBILITY, HERE AND NOW

Living in the here and now is concentrating on the present in accordance with one's own nature. It is not ignoring the future, but a recognition of the ignorance of future events. Rather than an abandonment of responsibility, it is the full acceptance of who you are, where you are and what you are doing. Welcome to the here and now. Everything that you have experienced has been necessary to get you where you are now. If you think that you have been in a better place, stop looking backwards.

POSITIONING

Living in the here and now can be done without an investment in the status quo. Be aware that inherent in your identity is a high degree of adaptability. That should be your focus whenever you become attached to the place to which you have adapted. Making a drastic change to stay where you are always puts you in another place.

DIRECTNESS

There is always a choice in your course of action, although you may have been conditioned to believe otherwise. One of the best ways to decide which choice to make is to list all the alternatives that you can think of while bearing in mind that nothing is unthinkable. Divide those alternatives into two categories—direct and indirect. The latter represent those choices that require getting other people on your trip. The direct choices need only your action. If you can't find a direct course of action, rethink the entire situation.

PATTERNS

Everyone learns the same lessons. From a cosmic point of view, the same thing happens to everybody. Each individual has had experiences that taught him or her a lesson that had to be learned. If someone is stuck in a behavior pattern that provides little happiness, the pattern will continue for as long as is necessary to teach the individual what there is in that pattern that must be learned.

JERRY'S RELIGION

When Jerry was working toward an advanced degree in psychology, she attended an institution which had formerly educated only students of one particular religion. The change in the religious makeup of the student body caused "What's your religion?" to be one of the questions often asked of most new students. Jerry always responded to this query by saying, "Zen Baptist." Some people heard only Baptist and Jerry related to them at that level. Other people heard only Zen and Jerry found them to be more interesting. A few heard what Jerry actually said and those were the people that Jerry considered part of her peer group.

TROUBLE-FREE ACTION

Things were going so well for Giovanni that he had difficulty believing the reality he was experiencing. He seemed to have dropped all his hungup habit patterns and was acting in a way that he didn't quite understand. To avoid the "This-is-too-good-to-be-true" paranoia, he asked Omar what he could tell him about the purpose of his new way of relating to the world. Omar said, "Don't worry about it. When you can't see through your own actions, you are operating at your highest level."

PAY AS YOU GO

You are as free as you are willing to be. Each act of freedom is your choice. If you see the situation in terms of consequences from a personal point of view, you can determine the price of the act. The price may require that you change the image you present to the world, that is, change it in a way that makes it more like the person inside. The price may be giving up a burden that you have become accustomed to. Only you can determine the price, and only you can pay it. Trying to influence others so they will help pay the price for your freedom will rob you of it. Act directly. Experience life directly. That way you pay as you go and live in freedom. Continued use of your freedom can free you of the urge to control others. You may become free of the urge to change yourself.

BOB'S ENLIGHTENMENT

Having gone through a number of psychological and metaphysical changes, Bob felt that he was very different from most people he encountered. His acquaintances all seemed to be preoccupied with the distinctions between them and him. Finally, Bob began to believe that he was so strange that even people he hadn't met could detect an alienness about his appearance.

To escape from this set of circumstances, Bob moved to a different city where he knew no one. Seeking employment, he went into an agency. As soon as he walked in the door, a man, who was talking with the manager, pointed at Bob and said, "He's just the one I'm looking for. Check him out."

The manager walked over to Bob and said, "Do you know your way around the city?"

"No."

"That's too bad. This man is a private detective and he needs someone to follow people. He's been here most of the day waiting for the right person, someone who looks anonymous and can easily lose himself in a crowd."

SKILLS AND TALENTS

Let your skills and talents be your servants, not your masters. Orient your efforts toward the realistic requirements of the existing situation instead of toward construing the requirements to be the same as your capabilities.

VISION

Ordinary vision would not be possible if the eye did not absorb light. Once the light has been absorbed, it is not seen again in the same form. This does not mean it ceases to function. One of the great uses for this light is self-illumination.

CHANGING TIMES

You are a process of change. Your cells renew themselves periodically, old concepts are replaced by new and your new being reflects life's experience. Flow with the changes. Be that new being. You don't have to make the person-you-used-to-be happy.

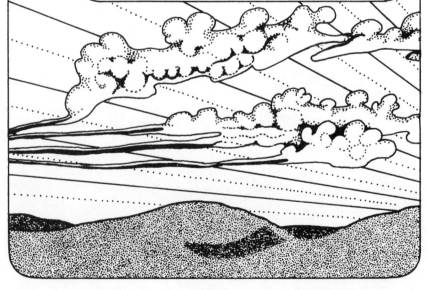

TAKING RISKS

Getting yourself in a position where you can't lose often puts you in a position where you can't win. Everyone takes a few risks in order to add spice to experiences. But the risk should always be gauged by what is wagered, not by what might be won.

GOOD VIBRATIONS

Like vibrations attract. If you are getting a lot of bad vibes in your life, put your attention on what you are transmitting. What you send is what you get.

PERSONAL EXPERIENCE

Knowledge is superficial unless it is accompanied by personal experience. Since superficial knowledge is an unstable foundation for a way of living, Zen stresses becoming one with your experience. Thus, Zen can lead to an understanding that the standard of living has little to do with the quality of life.

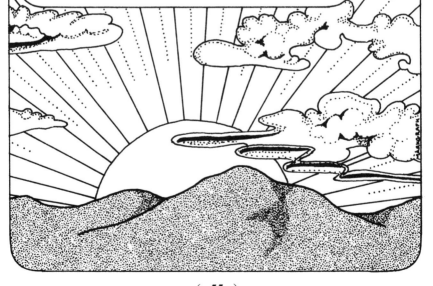

LUCAS'S SEARCH

Having been reared in poverty, Lucas aspired to middle class comforts. After gaining some education and experience with the world, he did not lose his taste for comfort, but realized how little he prized the middle class value system. Although he knew he could easily have one without the other, many of his acquaintances assumed that he aspired to both.

To liberate himself from what he considered middle class contamination, Lucas searched for a guru to guide him to a new level of consciousness. Ultimately he realized that spiritual advisers often tell their clients to give up all their worldly possessions merely because they are not capable of teaching people how to enjoy them without becoming attached to them. This realization led Lucas to the knowledge that his search for liberation must begin inside himself.

SUE'S PATH

Through meditation, Sue found an inner source of strength and determination. By using these resources, she changed her life into a series of events that brought her happiness and success. For her there is no conflict between orderliness and her free spirit. As she says, "I find freedom only through organization."

THE CIRCLE OF TRUTH

Once understanding has been reached—the understanding that ignorance will not guarantee the illusion of security—the search for truth can begin. But truth is not a constant. Like all other aspects of the greater reality, it is cyclic. A concept emerges from the great void as heresy, grows into truth, decays into superstition and returns to the void.

KARMA

Karma is the force exerted by a person's actions. It works in whatever manner an individual believes it does. In that sense all karma is instant—just add belief.

DOUBLE LEARNING

Everything that you learn about the world tells you how your brain works also, enabling you to perceive yourself in that which you consider "not you." A thorough understanding of this procedure will enable you to change the world by changing yourself.

INNER SPACE

When you are exploring the dark recesses of your mind, the people around you should be those holding the flash-light of acceptance. Sometimes you can recognize two qualities in these people—they know themselves, and they know that nothing is unthinkable.

DUAL FALLACIES

The subjective fallacy is: "If it works for me it will work for everyone." The objective fallacy is: "If it works for me I can get anyone to believe that it worked for me."

NO CREDIT, NO BLAME

Accept your positive experiences without taking credit and you have humility. Accept your negative experiences without blame and you have serenity.

ATTENTION

Your attention is a tool of your awareness. Your energy is like sunlight that you can focus by using your attention like a magnifying glass.

PAST BURDENS

The great value of the past is wisdom gained from your experience and pleasant memories. Everything else is excess baggage that handicaps the enjoyment of the trip. Yesterday's aches, pains and problems are not a burden here and now unless you brought them with you.

PATTERN DESIGN

Virginia's existence consisted of getting through one crisis after another, all of them self-induced. She became so skilled at kicking herself in the ass that she hated to give it up no matter how much it hurt her. Glowing with unhappiness and misery, she explained her bad karmic patterns to anyone who would listen.

Her co-workers tired of their consciousness-shrinking conversations with her. One of them prepared a poster for the office wall where Virginia would see it every time she began relating her troubles. It said, "Anytime you are in a pattern that produces unhappiness, you will continue that pattern until you learn the obvious lesson in it."

Design For Manually Operated Ass-Kicker

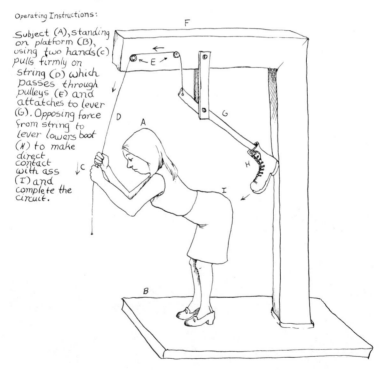

Operating Instructions:

Subject (A), standing on platform (B), using two hands (C) pulls firmly on string (D) which passes through pulleys (E) and attatches to lever (G). Opposing force from string to lever lowers boot (H) to make direct contact with ass (I) and complete the circuit.

GEORGE'S TEACHING

In Zen there is little emphasis on God or on Buddha because the focus is on becoming one with your experience. Anything that keeps distance between a person and his or her awareness of individual responsibility is a barrier to enlightenment. Even prayer can be a cop out. Or as George said, "Don't bother God. He's got his own problems—everything he makes dies."

COMING TO TERMS WITH DEATH

You who are reading or hearing this now will die. The death rate is a constant one hundred percent. Although the naturalness of death is basic, our cultural bias tends to treat it as an unexpected and foreign intrusion. If you embrace the concept that you will have your body as long as you need it, you can enjoy it. Rejoice in the fact that it is completely recyclable. The body has the wisdom that it is not needed forever. That wisdom can become a working concept in your life.

DIMENSIONS OF LIFE

The only dimension of life over which you have limited control is the length. By putting your attention on what you do to extend your life, you can utilize the potential you have for its duration. But be aware that every day you control the depth and width of your experience, your life.

MADNESS

The mad are persecuted because so many find it hard to love them. As for madness itself, it is the feeling that we can't love until we have time. Until we love, we will never have the time.

THE INMATES

When you first realize that you are surrounded by crazy people, it may seem frightening. In a civilization of outpatients, insanity can be viewed as the only defense. The planet Earth is your asylum; take the opportunity to explore and enjoy your own craziness.

JOANNE'S ENLIGHTENMENT

When her daughter was born, Joanne pledged to herself that she would not lie to her child. The discipline involved in answering the queries of an alert, intelligent youth was more than Joanne had anticipated. Nor had she realized that to fulfill her pledge she would have to stop lying to herself. By adhering to the truth, she went through many intellectual, physical and emotional changes that led her along the path of enlightenment.

THE NAMES OF HO CHI ZEN

Addressing a group of students, Ho Chi Zen said, "Heretic! Charlatan! Rascal! Trickster! I have been called all of those names and they're true. All true. I am here tonight to trick you. I'm going to trick you into becoming your own best friend."

III. The Zen of Sex

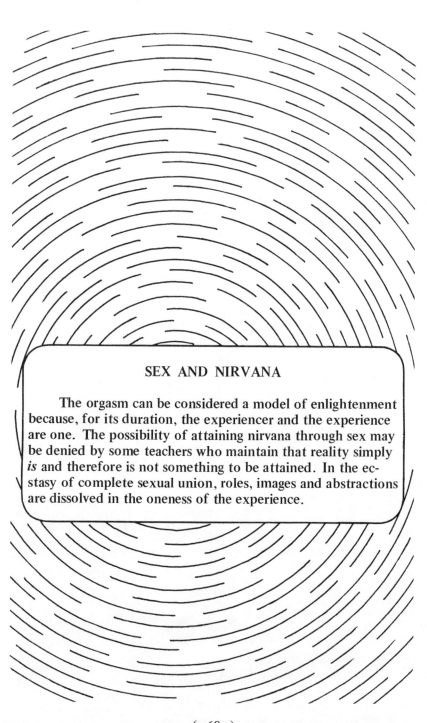

SEX AND NIRVANA

The orgasm can be considered a model of enlightenment because, for its duration, the experiencer and the experience are one. The possibility of attaining nirvana through sex may be denied by some teachers who maintain that reality simply *is* and therefore is not something to be attained. In the ecstasy of complete sexual union, roles, images and abstractions are dissolved in the oneness of the experience.

SEX AND MORALITY

An immoralist once fogged the issue of his own behavior by focusing attention on the sex life of others. This distraction worked so well that some people are just now realizing that morality is how you treat other beings, not your sexual behavior.

BEN ON HUMAN SEXUALITY

A student once asked Ben how to resist the animal in herself. Ben said, "That which is resisted persists. What are you resisting?"

"Well, you know, the animal passions."

"You mean sex?"

"Yes."

"That's so ironic. Most animals, except dolphins and humans, have a limited season of heat, of open sexuality. The constant readiness for sexual fulfillment is an unusual characteristic found only in species with large brains and high intelligence. Whatever it is, it is not animal passion. Your intelligence is so you can handle, enjoy and appreciate your uniqueness, not deny it."

JUD'S VISION

Jud founded a religious group based on sexual freedom; many members also enjoyed psychedelics. The combination of sex and drugs became a religious practice. Although detractors referred to this rite as total blasphemy, one believer said, "There may be a better way of worshipping than turning on and balling, but this will do until I find one."

When asked why he formed his group, Jud replied, "An angel came to me in a vision and told me that I was to be the next great religious prophet in this world. I asked the angel, 'Why me?' And the angel said, 'Because you are so goddamned gullible.' "

SEX AFTER LIBERATION

In a discussion about liberated sexual attitudes, Jerry explained that, to her, liberation meant using sexual activity to satisfy sexual desire. Through this framework she avoided being exploited or exploiting anyone else. One woman asked, "What do you do in a sexually free environment when someone accuses you of not being sexually liberated because you won't sleep with them."

"I tell him that I'm so sexually liberated that I make it with everyone who turns me on, and when I'm horny and there's no one around with the style I like, I feel perfectly free to masturbate without guilt."

CHASTITY AND OTHER PERVERSIONS

Pointing out that accepting oneself is a primary step in liberation, Ho Chi Zen advocated sexual freedom—doing what you want to do with those who are interested in doing it with you. One student asked why some gurus and prophets stressed celibacy as a prelude to enlightenment. Ho explained that such may have been necessary in the pre-birth-control era—just to keep the time for oneself that having children would require. That was why liberation was sought only after the child-rearing period was finished. "As for me," Ho said, "I agree with Anatole France who said that of all the perversions, chastity is the strangest."

WHAT IF EVERYBODY DID IT?

An unshackling of the spirit caused Joanne to exercise her sexual freedom and explore her sexual identity. When an acquaintance said, "You can't do that. What if everybody did it?" Joanne replied, "It's all right with me if everyone does it."

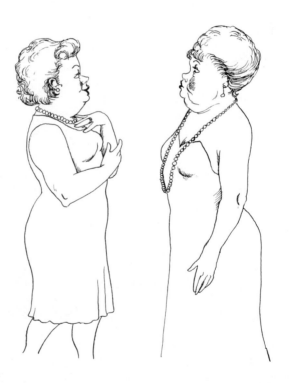

A CURE FOR PARANOIA

Rachel met Ed at a self-help lecture. Liking the way they responded to each other, they went out for coffee, then to Rachel's apartment where they shared a smoke of Acapulco Gold. Before much time had passed they were deep into each other's heads.

In response to Rachel's question about where he was coming from, Ed described the former life he had abandoned. During the description, he saw for the first time how full his life had been of form and how empty of substance. Seeing his past as a horror show brought Ed his first attack of paranoia.

Realizing what was happening to Ed, Rachel put her arms around him and pulled him close to her, saying, "That was then and this is now. That's where you were coming from, not where you are."

The warmth and closeness of Rachel brought Ed out of his revery and into the present. Sensing her emotional openness, Ed asked, "Are we going to make love?"

Rachel replied, "Of course. I'm no tease."

Ed's paranoia never returned.

JENNY'S LIBERATION IN ACTION

Among Jenny's lovers was a married man who was unaware of how chauvinistic he was. In order to avoid ridiculous complications, Jenny explained that she took responsibility for her own sex life and made love with whom she pleased when she pleased. Unable to grasp the implications of her freedom, her lover asked, "But what if I wanted a monogamous relationship?" Jenny replied, "I'd advise you to seek one with your wife—isn't that what she's looking for?"

ALBERTO'S INSIGHT

Because Alberto had not learned to believe in himself, he took pride only in those things he was born with—religion, ethnic heritage, skin color, etc. Thinking that he would find fulfillment by imitating the male role his culture pushed, Alberto became a stereotype instead of a person.

When the pressures of this imitation of life became too much to bear, he began searching for a better way to live. He studied Gurdjieff for a while, narrowly missed taking up Scientology and finally found himself in Zen.

One of his women acquaintances noticed the change in him and asked him how it came about. He explained that he had learned that machismo was Latin for insecurity in action.

BEN'S ROMANTICISM

Having been reared in a household full of logic and popular music, Ben was a romantic rationalist. His embrace of Zen didn't change his views, but widened them. When asked by Jane what his framework was for dealing with sex, he said, "I look at each sexual relationship as the possible beginning of a deep and beautiful friendship. If it turns out to be less than that, I accept the limitation although I don't prefer it."

Jane liked that approach, but said that so many of her friends seemed obsessed with monogamy. Ben replied, "Oh, I think monogamy is great as long as it's spontaneous."

HO CHI ZEN AND THE DRAGON LADY

Ho Chi Zen despaired of ever finding a partner whose enthusiasm for the Ten Thousand Imperial Acts of Sex would match his own. As soon as he gave up his search, a new partner appeared in his life; they discovered that they were astonishingly compatible.

After their first five days and nights of unstinting erotic activity, he said to her, "You are just what I always wanted, a Dragon Lady to fight by my side!"

She said, "But we have not conquered anything yet."

"Right on." Ho cried. "Perhaps we never will!"

IV. The Reality of Illusion

REALITY

In a discussion Bert said that reality can be described in many ways, but the description that an individual accepts is the one that conforms to that individual's preconceptions. Omar expanded on this by defining objective reality as the fantasy that has received the majority vote and subjective reality as a personal fantasy. Mal concluded the discussion by saying, "Reality is the original Rorschach."

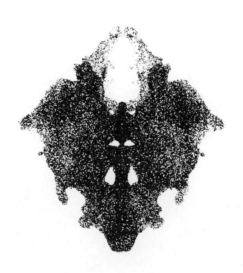

GOOD NEWS, BAD NEWS

There's good news tonight. And bad news. First, the bad news: there is no good news. Now, the good news: you don't have to listen to the bad news.

ILLUSION AND REALITY

Expounding on his knowledge of gurus and their systems, Ralph said, "Any system that prepares you for enlightenment by a description or a nondescription gives you the tools to build the illusion of enlightenment. If this is done with skill, it is perhaps impossible to tell the difference between the illusion and the reality."

Lucas replied, "Perhaps there is no difference."

ZEN SENSE

Everything is true in some sense, false in some sense and meaningless in another sense. A working knowledge of this concept is a useful tool for staying relaxed. For example, if someone says something about you that is untrue, you should not get upset regardless of whether you consider the statement positive or negative. It is true in the sense that it is what one person believes to be true about you; it is that individual's truth. It is false in the sense that it does not represent your truth. It is meaningless in the sense that it does not change who and what you are; your identity is independent of others' opinions.

IDENTITY RISK

Among the masks and roles of your everyday reality there is a genuine human being living a life. Speak out. Ask for what you want—there are only two risks attached. The first is that asking will let both you and others know who and where you are. That is necessary for learning your real identity. The second risk in asking for what you want is that you might get it.

THE CLOCK

When Omar inherited a clock from his grandfather, he placed it in a prominent position on his bookcase, even though the clock did not keep accurate time. He enjoyed it and was not disturbed when it refused to continue running.

The clock became a focal point for conversation. "Hey, that clock isn't right, is it?" "Omar, your clock has run down." "Does this clock work?"

One day Omar told Giovanni that he was considering having the clock repaired, not because he wanted it to keep time, but because he was tired of discussing its inaccuracy. Giovanni went over to the clock, removed both of its hands, and wrote NOW across the clockface.

TIME ORIENTATION

The past is just a memory and the future is a guess. The point where they meet is the present, and it is the only place you exist. The address of where you live is eternally now.

OPEN SECRETS

All secrets are open secrets. Nothing is hidden. Nothing is revealed. People can only be told what they already know. Although they know, they may not be conscious of their knowledge.

IMAGINATION

Imagination, like logic, is a valuable but limited tool. No matter how much imagination you have, life is always much simpler than you could ever imagine.

CAUSE AND EFFECT

It is easy to pick any event that precedes another in time and define the first as the cause and the second as the effect. Such definitions may be difficult to disprove but that does not insure their validity. Sometimes such a combination will be presented as common sense when it is merely stupidity hardened into a bad habit.

BELIEF AND CREATION

Today I heard about a new thing called whatamores. I now believe in whatamores. If you can belive in whatamores and if we can form a mutually acceptable definition, we will discover large amounts of circumstantial evidence proving the existence of whatamores. When we believe enough, there will be whatamores. Do we really want any?

SCIENCE AND MAGIC

Science and magic are frequently different maps for very similar territory. Following the path of least resistance, science ignores magic's hard-to-travel path. Magic uses myth and science uses ambiguous terminology: Semantically, both say the same thing. Each principle is expressed as "An unknown something is doing we don't know what." Each law is a variation of, "It did it again."

KEN'S TRUTH

Endowed with a psychic gift, Ken was able to determine
what kind of an emotional space a person was in by any physical contact. The experience happened every time he touched
someone, regardless of whether he wanted the experience or
not. Looking for a way to dampen the unpleasant aspects of
his talent, Ken became a heavy drinker. When alcohol failed,
he went to tranquilizers and then to heroin, to avoid living
his life.

After a number of years as a smack freak, he went into
a rehabilitation program to cure himself. Successful at last,
he left Synanon and began making his own way in the world.
As he expressed it: "What I had to learn was to associate only
with those people who I felt comfortable touching."

A MYSTICAL EXPERIENCE

Just as Mary was beginning to lose consciousness on an operating table, she received an illuminating glimpse into the essential nature of things. With a prodigious effort, she mentally summed up her fantastic insight in a dozen or so words, which she shouted to the white-masked faces around her before going under.

When Mary came out of anesthesia she could remember neither the words nor the vital truth they had expressed. She asked her doctor, "Did I say something just before I passed out?"

"As a matter of fact you did," the doctor told her.

"What *was* it?"

"Well, you just sort of mumbled. Nothing coherent. None of us could make any sense out of it."

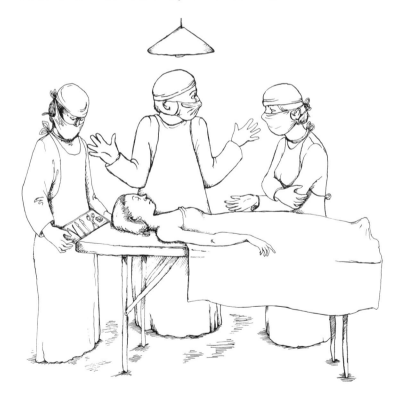

WISDOM WITHIN

You contain myriad worlds and vast knowledge. Each one of your cells has the ability to recreate itself and the ability to change. Although many of the processes that take place within you do not seem to be under your conscious control, that does not negate the fact that they are part of you. Your ordinary consciousness is a small part of your being, merely a current majority opinion resulting from your experience. If you invest your identity in your opinions, you are limiting your capacity and your reality.

SOLVING THE MYSTERY

If life seems to be a mystery, the solution is in your mind. It may not always be easy to find the solution but it is there, perhaps hidden or disguised in symbols or myths. The truth of the Atlas myth is that each of us is holding up the world with our shoulders. For it is in your head that the world you perceive is created. Knowing that may be the first step in recognizing that the world is not a burden, but a part of you.

FREEDOM AND THE LAW

All of the laws that identify victimless crimes are the result of someone's anxiety. These laws don't limit your freedom, but necessitate caution when you exercise it. The great challenge in contemporary culture is being free without becoming the victim of other's anxiety.

LUNACY

To be called a lunatic is a compliment to anyone who recognizes a better position than the one taken by allegedly rational human beings. Therefore, if there cannot be lunacy for all, there should be at least equality for lunatics. To those who are accused of being on the periphery of the lunatic fringe, all things are possible. It is on the outer periphery of the lunatic fringe, beyond lunacy, where the cosmic mystery is unfolding.

INFLATION

It may seem, in times of inflation, that all prices are going up, but the price of living remains the same—death. It may seem like a high price to those who don't understand it, but it only has to be paid once, and never in advance.

ART AND THE ARTIST

Every human being is an artist; the work of art in question is the individual's life. Most artists have a problem knowing when they have completed a work, but if you realize that your life is your art form, you don't have that problem. Death tells you when you are through. It's nature's way of saying, "That's it. You've completed your work. Take it easy now."

V. Meditations and Exercises

BREATHING MEDITATION

The major requirement for breathing meditation is a straight, erect spine. It doesn't matter whether you sit in a chair, on the floor or on a cushion. Once you are seated, close your eyes. Wiggle your body until it seems centered. Then move in smaller and smaller circles until you feel centered with your spine straight in a line that goes to the center of the earth. Now move your chin back—not up or down—until your ears are in line with your shoulders.

With your body in position and your eyes still closed, focus your attention on your breathing. Notice the air flowing through the nose, down the throat and into the lungs. Feel the chest expand and the muscles below the rib cage rise. Notice the instant of stillness as the inhale reaches equilibrium before becoming exhale. Feel the air flowing out of the lungs, through the throat and out the nose. Feel the chest contract and the muscles below the rib cage fall. Notice the instant of stillness as the exhale reaches equilibrium before becoming inhale. That total poise at the top and the bottom of the breathing cycle is you.

In order to keep your mind on breathing, let all thoughts that come to your mind float away like the outgoing breath. Count each breath silently as you inhale and then exhale without counting. Visualize the number if that aids in keeping your attention on the breath. Each time you reach the count of ten, start the counting over. If your attention has wandered, bring it back to your breathing. If you have lost count, start counting over.

This meditation can teach you to focus attention and to develop calmness. It can be done anytime during the day for a period of twenty to thirty minutes. Once a day is the usual way. After several weeks of breathing meditation, the results should be sufficient to tell you whether or not you should continue breathing meditation.

MOVING MEDITATION

Moving meditation requires a private, quiet place with room to walk around. The meditator prepares by sitting quietly until surface calmness appears. Once this has been achieved, the meditation begins by slowly walking to the center of the room or area.

Centered, stand still for a moment. Then allow the muscles to move as they release their tension. Instead of sending commands to the body requiring movement, let feedback from the body be the moving message—like the adjustment moves that are made with little or no conscious attention when preparing for sleep or finding a comfortable position on furniture.

Neither block nor encourage thought during the moving meditation. Because the emphasis is on letting any tension in the body work its way out, the exercise of the brain is not important during the movements. Relax into whatever motion seems to be what the body wants. Any movement made consciously, such as walking or turning, is appropriate provided it doesn't interfere with removing the tension indicated by feedback.

Relaxing the conscious control of muscles, let the body assume any position that is comfortable. Permit the vocal cords to relax and let any tension-reducing sounds emerge. Occasionally, let the head loll on the shoulders to loosen neck muscles.

During the meditation, any movement that feels right may be repeated while waiting for muscular feedback to generate. Moving from standing and walking to sitting or lying should be accomplished on a feeling basis. The emphasis remains on spontaneous movement.

By practicing moving meditation twice a week for a period of twenty to thirty minutes, most individuals lessen their muscular tensions and become more at home in their bodies. It can also be used as an aid in overcoming mental and physical discomforts produced by stressful situations. The benefits of moving meditation will be reflected in a greater awareness of the body and eventually a greater acceptance of the physical structure that houses the spirit. Those who continue the practice will notice that the subjective value of this meditation changes from time to time. The practice should be continued as long as the meditator finds dividends returning from the investment of time and energy.

WALKING MEDITATION

Whenever you are walking, concentrate on the body movements that you are making. Experience the physical flow as balance changes. Confine your attention to the feeling of walking and to the sensory input necessary to continue walking.

As you become one with your walking, the relationship between your steps and your breathing will become a familiar rhythm. The lengthening and shortening of muscles can be experienced as movements in the cosmic dance while your awareness moves through everything like a recurring theme.

See each walk as a process instead of a space between destinations. If your attention wanders, bring it back to the physical actions—the movements, the change in balance, the point at which the inhale becomes the exhale.

Becoming one with the experience of walking makes every step more satisfying. If you walk a thousand miles, each step should be as the first.

TRANSCENDENTAL MEDITATION

The techniques of transcendental meditation are deceptively simple. Twice a day at times when the stomach is not busy digesting food, the meditator recites mentally over and over a syllable or series of syllables known as a mantra for fifteen to twenty minutes. This should be done in a quiet place where interruptions will be minimal. The meditator should be nude or wearing only loose clothing and should assume any comfortable position in which the spine is straight.

If you are willing to invest approximately ten hours of your time over a two-week period, you can begin to discover what transcendental meditation can do for you.

Selecting a mantra is the beginning. Since the mantra will be recited mentally by you, it should feel comfortable to your mind. It should be something that evokes no particular chain of thinking or any special thoughts, because the mantra is used to quiet thought, to calm the mind. Any chant or word that your experience has led you to will do if it tends to produce serenity. If you wish, you may select a mantra from the following:

THE SPIRIT FLOWS FROM THE SOURCE
HA LA POU LA PLANE
TEA LEAVES
HOLLOW BAMBOO
OM MANI PADME HUM
ALPHA
THE JEWEL IS IN THE LOTUS
MANTRA
EEMO LEETOE LYTOE ZONYA
WHITE CLOUDS, BLUE SKY

Approximately two weeks is required to experience the benefits of meditation. Some of the more usual effects are increased energy, slight reduction in amount of sleep required, greater acceptance of the self and others, improvement in dealing with complicated situations and an expanded awareness. The subjective reaction to a particular meditation period is not always a reliable indicator of the value the meditator received from it. If, after a two-week trial period, you feel that you are not benefiting from the practice, discontinue it. It may not be the method or the time for you to practice.

Early morning on awakening and evening before the last meal or after it is digested are the two best times to use your mantra. With the stomach empty and the mind not under the influence of recreational drugs, mentally repeat your mantra over and over in whatever rhythm seems right to you. Anytime that you become aware that you are not saying your mantra, return to it.

There is no need to try to stop thought. Your thoughts are just the way your brain feels when it exercises itself in a certain way. Those thoughts have no more reality than you wish to give them. Don't think about your thoughts—just note them and let them pass on through. For instance, if you think "What shall I eat for breakfast?" during your morning meditation, you can follow that thought with "I am not eating breakfast now. Now is the time for me to recite my mantra." Then you mentally recite your mantra again and again until the meditation period ends.

Keep a clock or watch where you can see it. During meditation your eyes will be closed, but you may open them to help gauge the time. After a while, clocks will not be essential to judging how long you should meditate. When the time is up, arise slowly as if returning from a deep sleep.

Be assured that what happens during meditation is normal for you. When you have quieted the chattering of the mind with your mantra, you have gone beyond the conscious mind and may experience the equivalent of a dream. Accept the experience for what it is and for what effect it has on you.

If you feel sleepy after your meditation, sleep unless you have something more important to do. Frequently you may find yourself in a place similar to that threshold between waking and sleeping; it is a comfortable spot if recognized as such.

You can meditate alone or in a group. Having others to reinforce the positive experiences can be an aid in forming the meditation habit. Don't slip into the trap of using your meditation period to control the behavior of others by making them feel guilty if they disturb you. You are in charge of yourself and can return to your mantra when the disturbance is over. If your residence has few periods of quiet, meditate in the morning by awakening earlier and meditate at night before you sleep.

The values of transcendental meditation have been documented by scientists, philosophers and religious leaders, but only you can demonstrate them for yourself. The techniques are simple and readily available. Invest ten hours in yourself during the next two weeks and see what dividends you receive.

DAILY EXERCISE

Live this day fully. Keep your attention on what you are doing and what it means to you. Live entirely in the day you are experiencing and become one with the experience. If you find yourself lost in either the future or the past, return to this day. Live this day only.

BEING EXERCISE

You control the depth and width of your experience. The apparent limits of where you go, whom you associate with and what you do are largely of your own choosing as influenced by your heredity, environment and experience. This exercise will help you explore your own culture, different subcultures within it and other cultures.

Pick a cultural territory for exploration. Use your own resources for accumulating the information you need for your adventure. Then, dressed appropriately for the new environment, go into it and blend into the surroundings as much as possible without compromising your inner nature. Learn as much as you can from the experience.

CANDLE EXERCISE

You will need a person to help you in this exercise. Light a candle and place it a few feet in front of you. Look at the candle flame and place your attention there. Don't be distracted by random thoughts or by anything else that is happening in nearby spaces. Focus all your attention on the flame.

Every minute or two, at random, the other person will break silence to ask, "Where are you?" Don't give a verbal response. Just notice where your conscious attention is. If it has wandered away from the candle flame, bring it back. Repetition of this exercise will help you learn to focus the attention of your mind.

DECISIVE EXERCISE

If your decision-making processes have gotten so complicated that they are displacing the spontaneity in your life, this exercise can be used whenever needed to combat the long periods of worrying over choices. Use the CAN technique for difficult decisions. The C represents chronological choice; A is for alphabetical and N for numerical. When deciding becomes troublesome, tie a CAN to the choices. Since C comes first, use the standard of chronology, the measurement of time, to decide. This simply means doing whatever comes first in time. This means that you would take the choice that has the earliest starting time. If the choices all involve the same time, apply the alphabetical standard and take the choice that would be first if all possibilities were listed in alphabetical order. If the alphabetical system does not apply, rank the choices by numerical order—lowest number first—and take the first choice. If the choices don't have numerical values, use any number associated with them or assign a number according to any value system that you have. You can be a decisive person. You CAN do it.

ENERGIZING EXERCISE

Extend your arms forward, straight from the shoulders with palms down. Curve the fingers upward as far as they will go. Imagine that a tennis ball is bouncing against the palm of each hand with a regular, fast rhythm. While breathing deeply and regularly, clutch and release the tennis balls hitting your palms. Each clutch should press the fingers tightly against the palms; each release should return the fingers to the upward curved position. Make the rhythm as fast as possible and mentally count each time the fingers touch the palm. A count of fifty is the minimum necessary to get the feeling of energy that will help keep you alert and pay attention to whatever task is at hand.

HANGING LOOSE EXERCISE

Imagine that you are suspended by a single thread attached to your head as if it were an extension of your spine. Stand and shift your weight without lifting your foot until you have a good feeling of your line of gravity. Since the imaginary thread is attached to the head and not the face, you can let all the facial muscles respond to gravity—keep them that way unless you are using your mouth for talking, eating, drinking, etc. Your shoulders should hang loose except when you are carrying something. All the time that your hands and arms are not in use they should be limp enough to swing and dangle. Keep just enough rigidity in your legs and feet to give you support. Continued use of this exercise will help you to hang loose in your daily life.

RELAXATION EXERCISE

Getting uptight is always accompanied by muscle tension, a sensation that prevents rest and sleep. The way out of that tense feeling is to get into it, understand it and let go of it. Curl your fingers into a tight fist and sense what your muscles are doing. As soon as you identify the sensation, let your fingers uncurl and your hand go limp. The feeling of relaxation that comes as you let go is under your control.

Practice with the large muscles in the limbs and torso before following the same procedure with the smaller muscles around the face and throat. The longer you maintain a relaxed state in the muscles you have let go, the more the remaining muscles will tend to relax.

Develop your own sequence for relaxing your muscles. Use your developed technique to relax yourself whenever you get uptight. This symptomatic treatment won't prevent your getting upset, but it will help you spend less time being uptight about having gotten upset.

GIVING EXERCISE

With someone you enjoy touching, perform a body massage. Start with a thorough scalp massage. Make every movement firm but gentle, complete and without surprise. Use long, connecting strokes whenever possible. If oil or lotion is used, warm it in the hands to body temperature before applying. The hands should always return to the last spot they left to start the new stroke. In that way the person being massaged will not be startled by an unsuspected touch. Keep conversation down to the comfortable minimum, which may well be no words at all. All motions should emphasize the continuity of the skin. Help the other person experience their skin as the organ that connects them to the rest of the world instead of a shield that separates them from it.

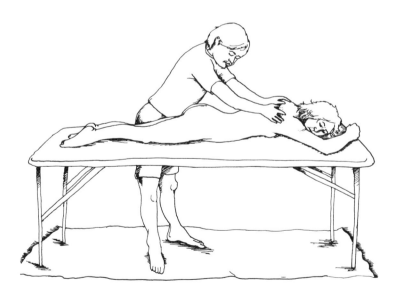

VISUALIZATION MEDITATION

This meditation is to be used to induce a feeling of calmness or to prepare you for restful sleep.

Make yourself as comfortable as possible before closing your eyes. Then imagine a scene that is pleasing to your mind's eye, a scene in which no people are present. The scene can be your recreation of a painting, your remembrance of an actual setting or something from your imagination.

Once you have picked your scene, go over it in your mind as if you were constructing it or painting it as a work of art. Imagine yourself able to work at any speed you desire with unlimited talent, time and materials. Use your own creation as a place to focus your attention, a place where you can always spend a few minutes relaxing and creating inner peace.

LIVING EXERCISE

Imagine that your life is going to be taken over and lived by a person who will be your best friend. In taking over, the friend will also take over your characteristics and beliefs in order to really live your life. As soon as you have imagined that, start putting your life in order for your friend. Get the garbage out, both physical and mental. Really shape up your life in the way that only you can. After all, you wouldn't want to put your best friend on a bum trip, would you?

LOVING EXERCISE

For one day treat everyone you encounter as if he or she were an enlightened being, doing whatever is necessary to raise your consciousness to a higher level. Suspect everyone of the very best of intentions. Anytime that you get uptight, use the energy that would be used in that uptightness to create. Create a new you who doesn't get uptight or a new situation wherein no one gets uptight. If you love everyone as much as you can no matter where they are or what they appear to be doing, you will be able to love that part of you that is so much like them.

HONESTY EXERCISE

Practice being honest with yourself, honest about what you feel, think and sense. Do not trap yourself into the habit of convincing yourself that you are as others see you or want to see you. Throughout your life you have been exposed to conditioning that has attempted to make you deny your feelings, thoughts and sensations. Relax and feel what you feel because it is real. Remember that nothing is unthinkable. Recognize your senses as a way of relating to your experience instead of selecting what is accepted or denied. When the practice of honesty becomes familiar, extend it to other people without using it as a blunt instrument. Continue this exercise until you find yourself being honest within the entire scope of your existence.

INVITATIONAL EXERCISE

For a two-week period, pay a great deal of attention to all the invitations that are extended to you. Accept every one that does not obligate you to a course of action you oppose or obligate you to commitments that you do not want. Write down all your invitations and whether or not you accepted.

This period should help you recognize many aspects of yourself. You will learn from the invitations you accept and from the invitations you decline. At the conclusion of your fortnight of acceptance, review your written list of invitations and decisions and examine the experiences you had. Then decide whether or not to continue the exercise.

LAUGHING EXERCISE

With a group of people seated in a circle, have one person start by saying ha. The person on the left should then say ha. When the ha has been said all around the circle, the originator should then say ha ha and the procedure be repeated. Continue the repetition with an additional ha each time the circle is completed until the process produces genuine laughter. The experience can be taped so it can be shared with others or played at random intervals.

FREEDOM EXERCISE

Each day you decide if you are going to be the same person that you were yestereay. Only you know whether the habit patterns, lifestyle and activities of that person you were yesterday are right for today. You can continue them, or you can make changes. The choice is yours—exercise it today.

QUESTIONING EXERCISE

The first step toward getting useful answers is framing useful questions. If you have experienced getting answers that were difficult to deal with, it may be that you aren't asking the right questions. Ask yourself questions like "Am I getting what I want from this situation?" "Should I continue doing this if it is merely a habit?" "What results am I getting from the expenditure of my energy?" "Are my actions in my own best interest?"

Pay attention to yourself and pay attention to what you learn from your questions. As you repeat this exercise, your questions and answers will become more meaningful. Remember that just as nothing is unthinkable, nothing is unquestionable.

SEXUAL EXERCISE

Do whatever you normally do to prepare the place where you live for an important visitor. Make the place as attractive as possible. Light candles, burn incense, provide the best smokes, pour the best wine and put on interesting music. Use your imagination to create a pleasing environment. The important visitor is you.

With two or more mirrors make an inventory of your nude body. Don't compare your body to any other person or structure, but view yourself as an abstract sculpture. Find and admire the attractive aspects of your body. You may discover beauty in the curve of a fingernail, the smoothness of a muscle or the contour of a rib. Examine all your body, every freckle, mole and hair. Find the attractiveness in your body that you never sought before.

Physically explore your body, using a lubricant such as oil or Vaseline—some substance that won't break down under friction. Discover what spots respond to a light bit of scratching or pinching. Vary the intensity, the motion, the direction and everything else. Learn what kind of reactions stimulation can provide. Every sensitive spot can be a turn-on under the proper stimulus. Continue the exploration until you have as much of this pleasure as you want. Don't ignore any part of your body. It's all there for your pleasure.

The final part of this exercise is masturbation. Not the hurried activity that quickly leads to a rushed orgasm, but a slow stimulation with occasional pauses to establish plateaus of excitement that stop just short of orgasm. Concentrate on the pleasure of approaching the climax; stimulate yourself until the feeling of orgasm tells you that you are almost at the point of no return, and stop. Resume when the feeling has subsided. Repeat the stimulation until you feel that you have reached a greater level of excitement than you have ever achieved previously. Now you know what turns you on. Now you can show or tell someone else how to turn you on. Now that you are turned on to yourself, you can guide yourself to the climax of this sexual exercise.

GARDEN EXERCISE

Perhaps you have seen a Zen garden or pictures of Zen gardens with the artfully arranged rocks emerging from smoothly raked patterns in the sand. If you have not experienced the serenity that such a sight can create in you, do so as the first part of this exercise. The second part of the exercise is to create in your mind a Zen garden of your own design. Create it slowly, selecting the shades of sand, examining the contours of each rock, making the placement of each item a ceremony of pleasure and satisfaction. Mentally rake the sand to leave the flowing patterns that delight the eye and direct the attention to the harmony of the creation. Develop the garden so that it delights the eye from any angle.

Once you have created your mental Zen garden, you may wish to create one in reality, using whatever materials are easily obtained. You might wish to create one in miniature using salt as sand and a small box as the container. Let your imagination be your guide—you might find a Zen garden in the yard more desirable than a traditional lawn.

Regardless of whether or not you create a Zen garden in the material plane, the Zen garden of your mind will always be available to you as a quiet place where you find the calmness that refreshes the spirit.

GETTING EXERCISE

If you feel that you are not getting what you want out of life, this exercise should help you get in touch with the causes of that feeling and lead you to a more positive state of mind. List on paper, in any order as they occur to you, all the things that you want out of life regardless of whether they are concrete or abstract, material or spiritual, emotional or intellectual.

When the list is as complete as you feel like making it, start refining it by getting rid of those items that are not within your personal sphere of influence. As an example, world peace might be on your list as something you want for the world. If it is, draw a line through it because it requires the entire world to get on your trip. Replace it with something that is personally meaningful—such as a desire to be at peace with the world or a desire to do all within your power to add to the amount of peace in the world. Delete all desires that require changing the past and substitute goals that require changing your attitude to what is past or changing your attitude to present conditions. If neither of those changes seems appropriate, list your desire to work toward changing the existing conditions. Eliminate all those ends that require specific action by other people because you can dissipate the energy you need to achieve your goals by expending it attempting to influence others. Next, examine your material wants, keeping in mind that ownership without use is material abuse. Free yourself from wanting anything that would complicate your life without giving you the return of usefulness.

After you have used your abilities to prune the list of all that is inappropriate, put the remaining items down in order of importance. These are the things you want. Now you know where to focus your attention and where to expend your energy.

At whatever intervals seem appropriate, review and revise your list. Add any item that you are sure belongs there and cross off those achieved or no longer desired. Maintain the list for as long as it is useful in helping you get what you want.

PAIN-EASING MEDITATION

Buddha recognized as one of his noble truths that suffering exists. Some suffering is the result of mental attitudes and can be alleviated by working on those concepts, expectations and desires—all of which can be changed. Other pain is a purely physical sensation and that is the pain that can be eased by this meditation.

Some of your response to physical sensation is conditioned, learned behavior based on past experience, present conditions and mental constructs. For example, a squeeze of your hand by someone who cares for you will usually be interpreted as a pleasurable sensation while the same amount of pressure as an expression of anger may register as pain. An awareness of this classification procedure will help you deal more directly with the physical sensations you experience initially as pain.

When you have a feeling that you have classified as pain and you have tried to ignore it unsuccessfully, turn your attention to it. All meditation is the controlling of attention. Focus on the pain completely and examine the sensation. Breathe deeply as you concentrate in slow, measured breaths and experience the stimulus. Experience the pain as something you have chosen to identify thoroughly. If it is not so great as to cause you to lose consciousness, this meditation will help you accept the sensation as a reality until you can change the reality that produces it.

PLEASURE EXERCISE

Every day do at least one thing that is intended solely for your personal pleasure. To get the most possible pleasure from the activity, make certain that it doesn't decrease the pleasure of others. Take responsibility for adding to the amount of pleasure in the world by pleasing yourself. Keep working at this exercise until you can fill an entire day with pleasure.

SECRET EXERCISE

Every day make an effort toward making someone else's day proceed smoothly. Do it in such a manner that your participation is unknown. Enjoy the experience of being an anonymous benefactor. If you are discovered, you can regain your anonymous standing by doing the exercise twice more that day.

SILENT EXERCISE

If you use any recreational or social drug, experience it the next time alone. Arrange the setting so that you will not be disturbed. Remain silent during the time that *' ɛ drug is in your system. Become one with the experience and learn as much as possible from it.

LIBIDO EXERCISE

This exercise is based on the old Tantric-Taoist sexual practices of prolonging sexual intercourse while avoiding male orgasm. Such a technique, sometimes called karezza, is often made ridiculously complicated with arbitrary requirements and technical divisions of continuing actions. Sexual intercourse prolonged can be a valid meditative technique, but there appears to be no viable reason, other than as an ineffective method of birth control, for not completing the act with eventual ejaculation.

The broad principles of getting the most out of the sexual encounter are extensive foreplay to excite both partners, a willingness to experiment, and pauses as required to delay the male orgasm. Additional helpful instructions are: Take your time. Keep your mouth closed unless you are sucking or tonguing. Make noises such as groans and shouts only when you can't prevent them from occurring. Avoid working yourself into a sweat. Be open to a wide variety of positions. Always be prepared to discard any rule or principle for the sake of spontaneity.

Exercising the libido is more a matter of approach and attitude than specific techniques. It is a contemplative form of lovemaking and mutual exploration that lets the lovers experience the neural, glandular and psychological sensations of the union.

PHYSICAL EXERCISE

Just as you are responsible for your mental programming, you control your physical programming. Your body responds to the physical activities you regularly perform by developing the ability to perform those tasks with greater ease. If you feel the need for more physical exercise in your life to enable you to accomplish physical tasks more readily, then it is your responsibility to incorporate that activity into your life.

If calisthenics, gym workouts, regular running or standardized exercise programs work for you, even if you are a superb physical specimen, you can still benefit from a personal physical exercise program. Start by determining what physical tasks are necessary or desirable in your life that are currently being performed by someone else or by technological means. Begin a program of doing these activities yourself to the extent that such actions are compatible with being the person you are. Be ready for the changes and flow with them.

Add to your physical activities by accomplishing tasks devised by you for your own enjoyment. If you live in a rocky area, you can move the rocks into your own conception of a rock garden. Perform those chores that will give you the bodily satisfaction of accomplishment. Doing your own physical labor can be as satisfying as doing your own thinking.

REPROGRAMMING EXERCISE

Since change is constant, you do not have to be the victim of past programming if you are willing to accept responsibility for your own programming. The circumstances of the past that created your existing behavior patterns do not have to be the circumstances of the future. Your reactions can change as easily as the circumstances if you are willing to take an active role in your life.

Examine your own programming for habits that are counterproductive, for preferences that are apt to become addictions, for reactions that are inappropriate responses to the situation. When you find the behavioral characteristic that you want to change, you have taken the first step toward meaningful change.

Once you have identified the bit of programming that you are going to revise, write down your intention to change. Add as much information as it seems worthwhile to describe completely the change you want to make. Then start collecting data that pertains to the change. Talk to other people who have made similar changes. Read whatever pertinent information is available on the subject.

The next step is imagining the new behavior response that you will have in place of the old. Make a mental film of yourself in the old situation with the new behavior. Play the film over and over in your mind until it becomes real to you. Then start living it with the joy of accomplishment.

INVENTIVE EXERCISE

All exercises are intended to keep your mind and body working in harmony with the life you have chosen to lead. You know more about that life than anyone else if you are paying attention to yourself. You are the one most capable of devising an exercise that will improve your existence. Invent one now and start it. Share the benefits with others.

RECOMMENDED READING

Browne, Harry. *How I Found Freedom in an Unfree World.* New York: Avon Books, 1973.

Cooper, Paulette. *The Scandal of Scientology.* New York: Belmont/Tower, 1971.

Golas, Thaddeus. *The Lazy Man's Guide to Enlightenment.* Palo Alto, Ca.: The Seed Center, 1971, 1972.

Keyes, Ken, Jr. and Burkan, Bruce (Tolly). *How to Make Your Life Work or Why Aren't You Happy?* Berkeley, Ca.: Living Love Center, 1974.

Keyes, Ken, Jr. *Handbook to Higher Consciousness.* Berkeley, Ca.: Living Love Center, 1973.

Laing, R.D. *The Politics of Experience.* New York: Ballantine Books, Inc., 1967.

Lilly, John. *The Center of the Cyclone.* New York: Julian Press, Inc., 1972.

Pearce, Joseph Chilton. *The Crack in the Cosmic Egg.* Julian Press, Inc., 1971.

Reps, Paul. *Zen Flesh, Zen Bones.* Garden City, New York: Anchor Books/Doubleday & Company, Inc.

Schmidt, Steven. *The Astrology 14 Horoscope: How to Cast and Interpret It.* New York: The Bobbs-Merrill Co., Inc., 1974.

Schmidt, Steven. *Astrology 14: Your New Sun Sign.* New York: The Bobbs-Merrill Co., Inc., 1970.

Sohl, Robert and Carr, Audrey, editors. *The Gospel According to Zen.* New York: Mentor Books/The New American Library, Inc., 1970.

Thompson, William Irwin. *Passages About Earth.* New York: Harper & Row, 1973, 1974.

Vassi, Marco. *The Stoned Apocalypse.* New York: Pocket Books, 1972.

Waters, T.A. *Psychologistics: An Operating Manual for the Mind.* New York: Random House, 1971.

Watts, Alan W. *The Book.* New York: Collier Books, 1966.

Watts, Alan W. *Psychotherapy East & West.* New York: Ballantine Books, 1961.

Watts, Alan W. *The Way of Zen.* New York: Vintage Books/Random House, 1957.

White, John, editor. *What is Meditation?* Garden City, New York: Anchor Press/Doubleday, 1974.

Weber, Nancy. *The Life-Swap.* New York: Dial Press, 1974.

Wilson, Robert A. *Sex and Drugs.* Chicago: Playboy Press, 1973.

CERTIFICATE OF
HOLY ORDINATION

BE IT KNOWN THAT

CAMDEN BENARES

HAS BEEN RIGHTEOUSLY ORDAINED AS A PRIEST OF
THE PARATHEO-ANAMETAMYSTIKHOOD OF ERIS ESOTERIC
AND THUSLY ENTRUSTED WITH ALL HOLY DUTIES
AND DIVINE PRIVELEGES OF THIS OFFICE

IN THE NAME OF THE GODDESS ERIS
GLORY TO THE SACRED CHAO

UNDER THE PATRONAGE OF APOSTLE THE ELDER MALACLYPSE
BY THE OMNIBENEVOLENT POLYFATHER OF VIRGINITY IN GOLD
MALACLYPSE THE YOUNGER, KSC; HIGH PRIEST

HAIL ERIS! καλλιχτι ALL HAIL DISCORDIA

11 DAY OF THE SEASON OF ___cfn___ YEAR OF OUR LADY 3136

Dr. Ignotum P. Ignotius K.P.S.
OFFICE OF THE POLYFATHER, POEE HEAD TEMPLE, S.F.
JOSHUA NORTON CABAL   THE DISCORDIAN SOCIETY

The Golden Apple Corps
HOUSE OF APOSTLES OF ERIS
THE DISCORDIAN SOCIETY

SECURITY LAST INTERGALACTIC
BANK OF MALACLYPSE
ENDORSED AND GUARANTEED

About the Author...

Camden Benares has been interested in Zen for a number of years. Preferring the informal approach, he sought out examples of how Zen worked for westerners in a western environment while reading everything he could find about Zen. In 1965 he joined the Discordian Society and observed Western Zen in the actions of Kerry Thornley, Gregory Hill and other Discordians.* He then began to have experiences, obtain insights and gather the information that eventually became this book.

In addition to the usual variety of occupations: Waiter, clerk, technician, theater manager, technical writer, alternative press editor; Camden had the typical variety of majors in colleges: engineering, business administration, theater arts, English. His avocation list includes disc jockey, civil rights activist, toastmaster, coffee house comic, lyrics writer, psychodrama actor, sexual liberation spokesperson, Zen lecturer, and meditation teacher. He lives with his wife in Los Angeles where he is currently doing both technical and freelance writing.

*The Discordian Society was a San Francisco-based dadaist, aesthetic-theological society whose stock in trade was esoteric satire.

New Falcon Publications

Invites You to Visit Our Website:
http://www.newfalcon.com

At the Falcon website you can:

- Browse the online catalog of all of our great titles
- Find out what's available and what's out of stock
- Get special discounts
- Order our titles through our secure online server
- Find products not available anywhere else including:
    - One of a kind and limited availability products
    - Special packages
    - Special pricing
- Get free gifts
- Join our email list for advance notice of New Releases and Special Offers
- Find out about book signings and author events
- Send email to our authors (including the elusive Dr. Christopher Hyatt!)
- Read excerpts of many of our titles
- Find links to our author's websites
- Discover links to other weird and wonderful sites
- And much, much more

Get online today at http://www.newfalcon.com